Praise for *H*

*"Like a hymn in pace and form, th
emotive liturgical summoning, dra
with such emotive passion, you
crucifixion."*

---Amy J--
Poetry Editor of Outcast Press
and Author of *Baptism by Fire.*

*"This book may seem like a punch in the face to some, but in
fact, it's just Joe, leaning his head on your shoulder and
aggressively whispering in your ear, 'Open Your Eyes!'"*
---**Jason Melvin**, Author.

*"Heresy is real, raw, and unapologetic. An honest look at
religion and the wounds it can leave, this work is dark and
personal and in-your-face."*
---**Perry Gasteiger,** Author.

*"In this collection you'll find poems that, if his words were fire,
your eyes would burn from their sockets."*
---**Sebastian Vice**, Author
and founder of Outcast Press.

The poem "Heretic" was first published by Outcast Press in a collection entitled *Falling Leaves and Flightless Birds*, August 2021.

The poem "Hope(Less)" was first published by A Thin Slice Of Anxiety, October 2021.

HERESY

JOE HAWARD

UNCLE B.
PUBLICATIONS
Indianapolis, Indiana

Heresy

Book Design & Cover Design by Tia Ja'nae

ISBN: 978-1-957034-06-5

For the abandoned and abused.
I hear you.

Table Of Contents

Introductions
Foreword by Sebastian Vice
Preface by Joe Haward

Part I: The Present Past

Part II: The Present Future

Conclusions

Foreword

I've had the pleasure of knowing Joe for only a few months. I met him on Twitter, but I can't remember the first interaction. What I do remember is the warmth he radiated, and there was something infectious about this man that stripped away my barriers. Alarms go off when someone is proclaimed to be a reverend (I've had most poor experiences with religious folks). I expected to be lectured at, talked down to, preached at, and dubbed a moral pervert. But this never happened with Joe.

Joe is a rare kind of Christian who, if I believed in the transmigration of the soul, would wager was Jesus of Nazareth. He has all the kindness of Jesus, and all the fire. His temperament reminds me of a Cornel West, someone who views us all as brothers and sisters in the most cosmopolitan of ways. He's the kind of guy who would sit with a strung-out drug addict, and not moralize or chastise. But he's also the kind of guy I imagine barging into a church, chasing out the hypocrites, and giving a scorching sermon.

Buddha isn't a name, or even a title. It's one who's woken up. It's one who's achieved enlightenment. I view the word *Jesus* in a similar way. Joe is Jesus. This doesn't mean he's divine. It means he mirrors and embodies the essence of Jesus.

It means he would, and has, done the things Jesus did. He sides with the downtrodden. And this is what makes him a heretic.

Joe takes seriously the message of Jesus, less so the bastardization of the message started by Paul and carried through various religious hucksters for power and profit. He cares about people more than institutions. And this makes him a heretic.

Joe treats people with dignity and respect, not about lobbying to oppress people. And this makes him a heretic.

While many, or most, churches follow the message of Paul, Joe follows the message of Jesus. Jesus wasn't a Christian. Joe might claim to be, but I've never thought of him in those terms. Joe is a follower of Jesus (not of Paul). And this makes him a heretic.

I don't want to make this intro too long, since you probably want to dive right into the poems as they are far more interesting than what I could say, so I'll end with this. In this collection you'll find poems that, if his words were fire, your eyes would burn from their sockets. What axe is he grinding? Institutional Christianity. I see this as a work of disillusionment, which I don't regard as a bad thing. Unpacking the word, it's removing the illusion. What's the illusion? Churches claim to follow in the footsteps of Jesus, but don't.

Jesus is the symbol to peddle bullshit for them, and Joe doesn't like that.

Joe is many things. A friend. A damn good writer. Most of all, Joe is Jesus.

Sebastian Vice
Founder of Outcast Press LLC

Preface

I am not anti-religion. Or, more specifically, I am not anti-Christianity; I am a Reverend after all (more on that in the Afterword). But *Heresy* is anti-institutional, an attack on the Church, and for that, I offer no apology.

Heresy is, in many ways, a deeply personal collection of prose and poetry. But it is also more than that; it is an unflinching attempt at authentic speech, with the explicit purpose to bring shock and outrage, as well as shine a light on the abuse, corruption, and hypocrisy of institutional Christianity. I have little doubt that it will upset some, make others angry, whilst some might even nod in agreement. But my desire, above everything else. is for it to be a moment of "somebodiness" where *Heresy* feels like someone's heart cry, a vessel through which you realise that you've been heard.

I use the term authentic speech rather than truth (although everything in here is 'truth') because all I can do is speak from the reality I have witnessed, experienced, and heard as an insider. This is a collection of authenticity, an unwillingness to look away or be quiet. Not everything in *Heresy* is directly to do with me (although some of it is), or people I know (although some of it is), but everything is based upon real lives and real stories.

After the final piece, we'll chat further, but for now, I need to warn you of what's coming. Some of the content contains references and allegorical language relating to child abuse, homophobia, racism, misogyny, and xenophobia. The language within this collection highlights the pain and injustice minorities, vulnerable groups, and those with little power, have endured at the hands of people with power and the institutions they represent. As someone that has experienced racism, both within and without the church walls, I wanted to give voice to those who have been discriminated against, abused, and hurt by these Systems of power.

When you've finished *Heresy* my hope is you'll feel heard and hear the cries of those who have been silenced. Then come and find me on Twitter @RevJoeHaward; let's talk and connect.

Joe Haward
October 2021

"The domination system is organised around a hierarchy of control, status and privilege. Routinely rights and freedoms are extended to those on the top and denied to those on the bottom. Such rankings limit thinking to two dimensions: superior or inferior; dominating or dominated."

---**Riane Eisler,** *The Chalice and the Blade: Our History, Our Future*

"Concepts create idols; only wonder comprehends anything. People kill one another over idols."

---**Gregory of Nyssa**

"Humankind exhausts, little by little, all illusions."

---**René Girard**

1.
Baptism

Drowning.

Dogma's dominance contrives cleansing, convincing brainwashed believers' beauty.

Alternatives avoided.

Asphyxiate.

2.
Disciple

Friendships exorcised
delivered from past lives.
New wine bursts old wineskins/skin crawling with
imposed regret.
Delight once tasted, tongue to tongue,
Shamed as penitent mouths wait for body and blood.
Flesh denied, blood running constrained,
Denied savoured pleasure for saviour's satisfaction.

"Repent!"
Weekly crucifixions of flesh and desire,
Surrender to Systems of pent-up tension.
(Un)Holy men (women not allowed) citing Scrip-
ture's commands.

Chapter and verse.
Subjugation's audiobook primed from pulpits,
Forced to suckle the nipples of power's persua-
sion.

Wrapped in fear's swaddling clothes,
Surrendering as peasants of knowledge. Self-
proclaimed wise men offer fools' gold.
Minds masticate myths' fabrications,
Knees bleeding
as body follows reason's suspension,
Doubt the sin of dictatorship.

Instincts crushed beneath the *Word*,
Identity squeezed between its lines,
Denial oozes across the page as the Self spills out.
Unblinking servants gather to slurp sycophantic
sewage,
Prevarication bottled as Living Water,
Truth's aridity scratches disciple's throats,
Revelation; the beginning of the end.

3.
Blinding Light

Renegade.

Rejecting myths sold for a dollar.

First light/Lost sight. Brainwashed in dogma's tales. A stench that clings.

Majestic stained, pane/pain stained innocents, hidden and silenced.

Heretics bleeding tears.

Forsaken.

Free.

4.
Heretic

"This is my body."
Surrendering to ancient desire
Sacrificial blood
Wine for venerated institutions.

"This is my mind."
Dampening dissent
Give them your brain
They bleach all critique.

"This is my strength."
Nothing more can be done
Weakness forsaken
You're better off dead.

"This is my soul."
Midnight's despair
Abandoned by the dogmatic curse
Fucked by heretic's thorns.

5.
Offering

Outcast
the refuse
and refused
sacrificed upon ideology's altar
rejected by dogma's dynasty
scapegoats
screaming
at institution
dehumanised
silenced by
pulpit's power
Fucked

6.
The Curtain of Oz

Community (cult)

Teaching (propaganda)

Faith (fear)

Worship (braindead)

Relationships (conditional)

Love (manipulation)

Questions (dissent)

Bible (god)

God (tyrant)

Prayer (gossip)

Justice (power)

Leader (dictator)

Rules (unbreakable)

Forgiveness (scapegoat)

Money (control)

Tragedy (growth opportunity)

Freedom (institution)

Marriage (handmaid's tale)

Church   (dead)

7.
The Desolation of Abomination

"We love you"
Warm hands caressing shivering bodies
Frightened faces downcast in surrender
Hell's fire warming blistered feet
Pacing grooves into midnight's floor
Praying for anything but this.

"Let's pray for you"
Sweaty hands laid upon shivering bodies
Desperate faces upturned pleading for deliverance
Hell's fire lapping distended tongues
Babbling ancient condemnation
Severing trust and safety.

"Christ compels you"
Forceful hands slamming bodies of regret
Screwed up faces clamouring together
Vociferating hellfire as judgement burns.
Disgust dribbling down self-righteous chins
Secret urges suppressed for the right to *rite*.

"Homosexuality is an abomination unto the Lord!"
Hostile hands cast out outcast bodies
Defiant faces unmoved underneath compassion's
desert.

Help burns
Bigotry's ash choking in the throats of fear
Demonic institutions rotting in the sulfur of their
own hate.

8.
My Child

"Happy shall they be

who take your little ones

and dash them against the rock!"

We delight as

the brains of our children are destroyed.

Shape.

Impress.

Mould.

Doctrine's rock ("on this rock, I will build my Church")

Young one,

let us smash your brains in,

we shall feast on the remains.

9.
Prosperity Gospel

Repent and believe in the name of the Lord and you will be saved/from the boredom of your existence as millions are made from gullible people/searching for salvation from a God who loves/you will be richer than you've ever known from insignificant hoards surrendering wealth for the promise/of God's blessing if you act in obedience to his will/swim in the abundance that your deception generates/possibility that only your tithe can unlock/taxfree banquet for preaching tantalising deceptions to people/repent and believe on the name of the Lord

and you will be saved.

10.
A New Creation

Standing in the water I hear promises ripple
across the air.

"Anyone who is in Christ is a new creation."

Fragile wounds spill out at event's gravity,
the offal of regret polluting the pool.

Maybe I'm making a mistake?

The preacher rhapsodizes,
ancient words resplendent in revelation,
plucked from the top shelf of masturbatory
congratulation.

"The old has gone! Everything is new!"

Previous passions have disappeared.

A miraculous eradication?

Like yesterday when I called her a fucking bitch?
Vodka's seduction surrendering senses,
a river of anger from drunken pores,
flowing into a familiar ocean.

Does my baptism wash away her pain?

Like a silver coin vanishing from the magician's hand?
(*It's still there you prick, only hidden, out of sight*)

I'm buried beneath the water,
Christ's death overlaid upon me,
a religious filter on self.i.e.
I'm an influencer,
revealing God's grace,
the worst of sinners redeemed.

For now, at least.

Rising from the water,
crucifying resurrection's promises,
hands nailing repeated punches,
her tears baptise swollen cheeks,
cracked lips wishing I was dead.

Washing the blood off my fists,
I leave for church,
but not before I sit in judgement,
reminding her that she needs Jesus,
otherwise she's going to hell.

Kneeling before the altar I thank God for eternal
forgiveness.

I am a new creation.

Interlude

"But the bank is only made of man. No, you're wrong there— quite wrong there. The bank is something else than men. It happens that every man in a bank hates what the bank does, and yet the bank does it. The bank is something more than men, I tell you. It's the monster. Men made it, but they can't control it."

---**John Steinbeck**, *Grapes of Wrath*

Somebodiness Perspective

Sex is beautiful.

A worker deserves their wage.

12.
I Thirst

My God,

my God,

why

have

you

forsaken

me?

Darkness stalks every waking hour

Despair crawls as blades under my skin,

severing joy

from my bones.

Self

peeled

back,

exposing the soul's bleeding corpse.

Help me

echoes off

stained glass ceilings,

religious abattoirs

for the mentally ill. Midnight desolation is the

only friend, doctrine dogmatically denying

depression's existence.

Heaven silently mocks, screams into chasm's

hopelessness,

punishing atheistic surrender.

13.
Welcoming the New Priest

Moving from home to home
Past lives erased
Buried and consecrated under the sign of the cross.

The stain of tears
Painted over and varnished
The stench of perfection's whitewash.

Innocent sobs muffled
Silenced beneath cassock and power
Institution rejoices over one priest who repents.

Cruel indifference Secrets and lies
Victims' collateral to protect ordained desire.
Quietly creeping into a new community

Fabricated Father masking evil intent
Smiles seduce whilst lives are destroyed.
Fuck you Father For you have sinned

Perhaps Satan will hear your confession.

"If anyone harms a child, it would be better for him to have a millstone hung about his neck, and to be drowned in the depths of the sea."
Jesus

14.
The Good Book

This is the Word of the Lord
Thanks be to God.

Dusty earth slick with blood and milk
As swords cut through nursing mothers
Burning flesh
Incense to a Holy God
Jericho
Ai

Canaan
Rubble and ruin

This is the Word of the Lord
Thanks be to God.

Whimpering cries through the night
Subjugated to patriarchal abuse

Her body; raped and destroyed
Cut into twelves pieces

Nameless
Silenced
Murdered
Rapacious ruin

This is the Word of the Lord
Thanks be to God.

Husband and wife lynched by the community
No chance to say goodbye
Labelled devil's own

The rules of a Holy God
Must Be Obeyed
Regime and ruin

This is the Word of the Lord
Thanks be to God.

15.
Gilead Part Two

Churchianity

Sex is evil.
Workers will burn in hell.

16.
The Walking Dead

Their mother had died.

Looking for comfort in the desolation of mourning
night you heaped cruel darkness over anguish-
stinging eyes.

Standing among the tombstones
they offered a simple question

asking if heaven beckoned the faithful and faithless
alike.

Staring into the finality of the grave's abyss
you preached hellfire

the certainty of torment and suffering
"A woman deserving of hell,"
your final words were spoken to grieving children.

You recount the story with pride
delighted by the horror
surrendered entirely to the ideology of hate.

It is then I realise
you are dead to me.

17.
You Belong To Us

We're new to the area.

You are welcome to join.

It's wonderful to make new friends.

How important it is to **Belong**.

Church is surprisingly friendly.

Commit **To** something more.

We only have you.

There is no you, only **Us**.

18.
Assimilate

"Are you in debt?"
Benevolent lives offer a path of salvation from
arrears.
(*youhavetocometochurchyouhavetocometochurchyouhavetocometochurch*)

"Are you hungry?"
Generous hands distribute food to starving stomachs.
(*youhavetocometochurchyouhavetocometochurchyouhavetocometochurch*)

"Are you cold?"
Blankets, soup, a bed, given as winter's bite grips.
(*youhavetocometochurchyouhavetocometochurchyouhavetocometochurch*)

"Do you have any friends?"
Invitation to homes, a film night,
(*Bible study*)
community.
(*youhavetocometochurchyouhavetocometochurchyouhavetocometochurch*)

"We love you."
Un
(*conditional*)
love, absorbed and welcomed into *ekklesia*.
(*we'vegotyouwe'vegotyouwe'vegotyouwe'vegotyouwe'vegotyouwe'vegotyou*)

19.
Communion

Body.

Bleeding brokenness

Craving caring community

Death driving desire

Entangled empty edicts

Feigning freedom Fear.

20.
Serpent

Taste, eat, the Lord is good.
    Fruit plucked from irreplaceable desire.
Satisfaction the sin of saints.

    Taste, eat, the Serpent soothes.
        Women   cursed   to   stain   the
ground.
Blood, water, breast milk, a poisoned chalice.

Boa de Natal (Hortulia Natalensis).

Taste, eat, suckle on the Church's nipples.
Saved within patriarchy's bosom.
Seamen the glue holding institution together.

Taste, eat, whisper holy men.
Tongues savour power's delight.
Bodies wrapped around unpalatable Systems.

Interlude

"To bring about change, you must not be afraid to take the first step. We will fail when we fail to try."

---Rosa Parks

"We are not to simply bandage the wounds of victims beneath the wheels of injustice, we are to drive a spoke into the wheel itself."

---Dietrich Bonhoeffer

"If we cannot recognise the truth, then it cannot liberate us from untruth."

---James H. Cone

21.
New Car

Final coins feel warm in sweaty hands
Anxiety prophesying the week ahead

Stomach crippled in present hunger
A single tear wets past regrets.

I tell you that I am poor
Rattle of change and bones

Desiring Communion bread and wine
A feast briefly quenching acidic starvation.

Remember the widow's mite you tell me
Giving out of her poverty

Kingdom's work and glory first
The Lord will provide your needs.

My lungs burn walking home from church
Breathing in smoke and fumes

Incense from your new car
As you wave and drive past.

22.
Exorcist

Fuck me, Jesus!
Priestly exultation.
A child's cry,
Smothered beneath ecclesiastical power.

Fuck me.

No.

Cast out.

Jesus, help.

23.
Jonah Lomu

Do you remember me?

We sat together one Sunday morning in church.

I was only small.

I don't suppose you noticed me.

You were laughing with your friend about the rugby player, Jonah Lomu.

Together you joked that in a dark alleyway Jonah Lomu would have to smile so that you could see him.

I wonder if you noticed my brown skin?

24.
Delight

Family.
Singularity of purpose.
Embraced.

Question.
Upsetting framed equilibrium.
Chastised.

Doubt.
The Devil's work.
Repent.

Denial.
The Judas equation.
Outcast.

Freedom.
Cherishing incessant cerebration.
Delight

25.
Anxiety's Curse

Kneeling on the floor,
body shaking with anguished fear, identity
determined
by theological fever.

Heavenly hallucinations render reason obscured,
enlightenment
fading
dawn's promise rendered faultily.

Fright
and
flight

scratches against windows of the soul, mirrored
terror
by ancient myth
scraping desperate throats.

She
looks
up,
tears falling in disorientated despair
voices murmuring demonic possession.

Prayers clamour for recognition

hands
and
lips

wet in a delusional frenzy. A fragile heart threatens explosion

anxiety's curse unrelenting.

26.
Preacher

A broad smile sustaining enraptured audience as clever phrases trip lightly off the tongue/licking the asshole of his twenty-five-year-old prostitute/was saved by Jesus as no-one is beyond his power/full of regret as orgasm pulses under laboured breath/ of the Spirit will give new life to those who repent of their/bodies slick with sweat from temptation's beckoning call/on the congregation to heed his warnings and embrace/cock into his mouth/that revealed pearl white teeth glinting in the lights/dimmed low hiding regret/is a sign that God is speaking/salacious words into his ear prompting a broad smile.

27.
#LoveWins

~~God has made us in his *own* image~~
~~male and female~~
~~and marriage is his gift~~
~~a holy mystery~~
~~in which man and woman become one flesh~~
~~united in love.~~

~~Husband and wife.~~

Love wins.

28.
Ten Commandments

And God spake all these words, saying,

I am the Lord thy God, which have brought thee out
of the land of Egypt, out of the house of bondage.

(into a prison shaped like a cathedral)

One
Thou shalt have no other gods before me.
(apart from money, money is acceptable)

Two
Thou shalt not make unto thee any graven image.
Thou shalt not bow down thyself to them, nor serve
them: for I the Lord thy God am a jealous God, visit-
ing the iniquity of the fathers upon the children unto
the third and fourth generation of them that hate me;
And showing mercy unto thousands of them that
love me and keep my commandments.

(bow to nation and flag,
to respectability and obedience,
to a quiet mouth and contrite heart,
mercy exists only in surrender)

Three
Thou shalt not take the name of the Lord thy God in
vain; for the Lord will not hold him guiltless that
taketh his name in vain.
(your name is invoked for men like Trump,
used to justify such moments of madness)

Four
Remember the sabbath day, to keep it holy. Six days
shalt thou labour, and do all thy work: But the
seventh day is the sabbath of the Lord thy God.
(church is the bastard of capitalism,
there is no rest)

Five
Honour thy father and thy mother: that thy days may
be long upon the land which the Lord thy God
giveth thee.
(no room in the Inn,
to honour LGBTQI+ parents)

Six
Thou shalt not kill.
(killing in the name of,
flag and nation,
acceptable blood on war's altar)

Seven
Thou shalt not commit adultery.
(prosperity preachers,
leaders of status
seducing the vulnerable)
Eight
Thou shalt not steal.
(take your life,
assimilate it into the System,
ransom it for institutional gain)

Nine
Thou shalt not bear false witness against thy
neighbour.
(depends upon who the neighbour is

Ten
Thou shalt not covet thy neighbour's house, thou shalt not covet thy neighbour's wife, nor his manservant, nor his maidservant, nor his ox, nor his ass, nor any *thing* that is thy neighbour's.

(your only desire will be the desire we desire)

29.
Gilead Part Three

Patriarchy Perspective

Sex is necessary.
Surrender to your husband's will.

30.
Judgement

Love the sinner
hate the sin.
Bullshit slogans designed to
hate the person
you've made a sinner.
Labels stamped
like 666
on souls you deem
marked for fire.

Interlude

"Unjust systems perpetuate themselves by means of institutionalised violence."

---Walter Wink

31.
Apocalypse

A great flame-hued dragon who had seven heads and ten horns and on his heads seven diadems.

A woman clothed in the sun.

The Revelation of John the Divine of Patmos.

Revelation.

Apokalypsis in Greek.
Unveiled.
Uncovered.

What did you unveil, John?

Did you find her naked
And shame her song?

Did you find the beast sitting on its treasure
The bones of the dead scattered around the cave?

Centuries pass.
Liberation's song fades.
The institution gorges
Adorned in gold.

32.
Fake

Teeth glistening under artificial lights
Vampiric desire as fresh blood arrives.

Unconditional love part of vision plan
SMART goals to increase weekly numbers.

Surfaces left unscratched to hide broken past
Idle tongues are a gift to community cohesion.

World's do not fall apart in manufactured utopia
Simulated satisfaction sustains the smile's facade.

Pain buried beneath a veneer of respectability
Teeth glistening under artificial lights.

33.
Monster God

"Eat my flesh."
Zombied Saviour.

"Drink my blood."
Vampiric Messiah.

"One body, many parts."
Frankensteinian Redeemer.

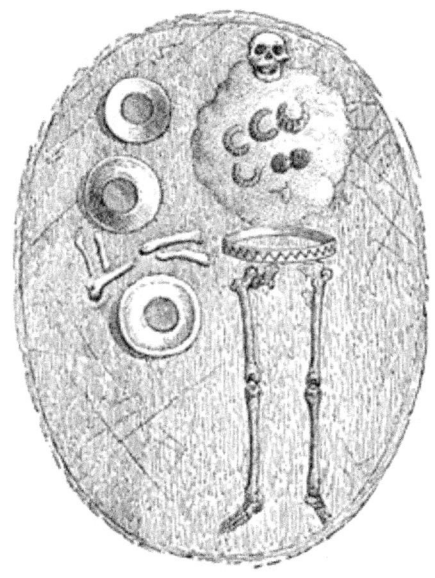

"Thirty pieces of silver."

Lycanthropic Deific Slayer.

So the Lord said, "I will blot out from the earth the hu- man beings I have created—people together with animals and creeping things and birds of the air, for I am sorry that I have made them."

Monster God.

34.
Sinner

"The Lord looks down from heaven
on humankind," he bellows,

sweat descends
blood red face rises.

"They have all gone astray, they are all alike
perverse!" Judgement reverberates,
nodding heads
minds blades sharpening condemnation.

"There is no one who does good!"
Not one, he insists
striking his wife's face

35.
Flat Line

Her skin – taut and stretched tight
translucent and pale
skull forcing bare necessity
hospital white lights painting a child's face
with a hellish ghastly glow.

Parents pray for saviour's touch
flayed by the will of God
trusting eternal Love for earthly remedy reduced to
the ash of despair.

Preacher claims healing power
declares the daughter of Jarius restored
calling for faith from fervent followers.

Hope's
stench
lingers
like a lover's promises to leave his wife.

Another child dies.

36.
Tent Revival

Gather round,
Gather round.
Wander from the farthest corners.
Wonders from the furthest corners.

Suspend your disbelief

Listen to my voice,
Prepare to be amazed.
Open your hearts.
(and your wallets)

The blind will see.
(look)
The deaf will hear.
(death was here)
The lame will walk.
(run)

Surrender your pride.
Join us.
A new life released from sin's chains.

(I once knew my life: help, I'm a prisoner

37.
Hope(Less)

Like the emaciated remains of a starving child, sifting
through the detritus of society's

fabricated longings, we stagger, hunger unable to
dissect

desire.

The illusion of dreams, asthmatic aspirations
wheezing on the polluted air of enlightenment. A
glimmer, seductively offering an inner thigh of
possibility,

a pathway towards sybaritic nourishment. Good
home, good grades. Good god, what happened.
Decrepit lives graffitied, hidden behind the nostalgia
of tomorrow's world. Possibility's potentiality
perennially postponed. Naked emperors sit upon
culture's lepers, sucking marrow from dead bones.

You can be anything you want to be.

Clawed fingers broken with yearning crawl through
corporations' filth, applauding power's perversion.
Mouths masticating crumbs from under the table beg

to suckle the drool from ideologues' chins, savouring
its bitterness. Feasting upon the vapidity of fool's
paradise,

there is never
enough
to go around.

38.
Snake Charmer

Primed by the persuasions
of
preachers and peddlers
selling
promises
to sickly desperate people.

Venom dribbles from predatory mouths
with the careless abandon of
devils.
"And these signs shall follow them that believe,"

frenzied voices vociferate
to
beggars and vagabonds, turning desire
on
a
dime
and
a
dollar. "They shall take up serpents,"
sermonizes snake-oil sellers to inveigle

captivated
crowds. "And if they drink any deadly thing, it shall
not hurt them,"

drips deliciously into dehydrated minds.

Fundamentalist venom poisons sanity
as

kleptomaniacs
suck up and spit out
rationality. Congregations sway to the movements and
music of charmers, madness manipulated
until

absurdity

commands

total control.

39.
Devil

The śātān
means Accuser in Hebrew.

I went to church today.

Pastor pontificating accusations against
LGBTQI+ community:

Everlasting hell burning society's deviants.

I went to church today.

Youth pastor the white-teeth-gleaming-accuser: The
devil's desires are rotting your wayward souls.

I went to church today.

Spittle flies from visiting preacher's accusing lips:
Women's bodies belong to men and God. How dare
they?

I went to church today.

Accusations choke the air of hospitable respect
ability.

Asylum seekers poisoning indigenous Empire.

The śātān

means Accuser in Hebrew.

40.
Jester

A crown of thorns
King of court's jester
Draped in Emperor's new clothes.

Seamen.
Spit.
Blood.
Bile.
Crusted within torn beard.

Insatiable crowds
Mob's rapacious desire
Sucking order into the chasm of chaos.

The Church's Event Horizon
A moment traversing System's existence

Indomitability the path within collapse.
Surrender.
Nailed.
Bleeding out to Power's demands
Cleansing water from broken side
River's flow to loss of control
Salvation from sycophants and despots.

Authority's seduction shivers
The promise of domination
Ruling erection of anticipation
Empire's stones are laid
Blessed by priestly hands.

The court Jester weeps.
Blood from his crown
Despairing eyes sting
As awareness dies.

Interlude

"Number one in your life's blueprint, should be a deep belief in your own dignity, your worth and your own somebodiness. Don't allow anybody to make you feel that you're nobody. Always feel that you count. Always feel that you have worth, and always feel that your life has ultimate significance."

---Dr Martin Luther King Jr.

Afterword

By the age of twenty, I was an alcoholic. Over the years I have sought to downplay the reasons as to my alcoholism, convincing myself that it was simply a wild teenage pit that became an abyss I was unable to escape. But, as I have allowed myself the space to think upon my addiction, I realise that alcohol served as a form of catharsis to deal with an assortment of mental health pain.

With my identical twin brother, I was adopted as a baby at the start of the 80s. My birth mother is Indian, my birth family hailing from the Punjab and Assam regions of India (I recently discovered that part of my family heritage is also from Afghanistan). My parents are white, and the community I grew up in was white, a small fishing community that my family have lived and worked in for generations.

Racism was commonplace. Occasionally it was aggressive, moments where someone threatened you with violence, but more often it was delivered with a smile and a pat on the back. In British communities like the one I grew up in, people will, in the main, vehemently defend themselves against charges of racism. Yet the uncomfortable truth is that many British communities are steeped in racist and xenophobic attitudes where people of colour are dehumanised on a daily basis.

Throughout my childhood and teenage years, people used racist slurs against me, laughing afterwards as though it were a harmless joke. When I was seventeen, a friend of mine sang a racist song about me for the entire bus journey home, laughing with delight as others smiled and joined in. When racism happens with such regularity, you become desensitised to it, accepting it as 'normal', simply the way things are.

But it leaves a mark.

Extreme financial hardship also followed us as a family. Without going into the gritty details, such economic strain is painful, and lives are pulled to breaking points. When the devastation is so severe, parents cannot hide it or protect you from it. There is a raw terror to such instability, one that daily reminds you how grey the days have become. No doubt you try and make the best of what you have, hoping for a better and brighter tomorrow, but it leaves a mark.

Drinking masked the daily terror I felt.

It can be difficult to describe, but there were mornings I would wake up and curl up in pain at the nihilistic devastation I felt. Some days I felt as though I was in a dream, floating in a state of unreality, never entirely sure if I was a real person. Alcohol became a shot of reality for me, the opportunity to feel something other than despair or the emotions of fractured consciousness.

The next drink became my entire life and existence, all-consuming in its power over me, all desire determined by its susurrations. People don't realise how productive you can be as an alcoholic, keeping a job going whilst drinking a litre of vodka a day.

Then I found religion.

It's a cliche, I know. But it happened.

I became addicted to the Bible.

At the time I felt like my whole life was falling apart, and then you hear that God wants to put you back together and transform your life. It's a powerful message for an addict.

I threw myself into church life, volunteering in any way I could, regularly wheeled out by the leadership to speak about my miraculous conversion experience. Within a couple of years, I was working for the church, tasked with growing the numbers and building the church's profile within the community. A year later and I'm training to be a Reverend.

Your life is filled with dogma, reality reduced to absolutes and fear of a god who will cast the immoral and the unbelieving into hell. And you work day and night trying to be a better person, continually aware that you're a piece of shit to god, a stain on existence that might get to heaven one day, if you're lucky. Each and every day is a ritual of prayer and Bible study, repentance and regret, working harder and harder for the church trying to earn the favour of god and god's people.

But it is never enough.

And it is addictive.

Then something breaks, or rather, clicks, and you start waking up.

Just as I became aware of my alcoholism, the power and poison it had upon my life, so too the same realisation came about the church. Within the walls of the church, I witnessed racism, misogyny, homophobia, transphobia, and hypocrisy. Indeed, I've witnessed the same beyond the walls of the church. But for so long I believed the church was meant to be an example, "a light shining on a hill," as Jesus puts it. What I *actually* saw was humanness sacrificed upon the altar of theology. How easy it is for Christians to walk away from relationships because of doctrine and belief. There was a shallowness and ease by which relationships ended and people discarded.

Heresy is filled with these moments of clarity.

My work and writing over the last two years has been about exposing the hypocrisy, corruption, and abuse of the church, speaking out as someone who is an insider. This book is one example of that.

Some of you might be asking, "Why are you still a Reverend, then?"

Good question.

Honestly? I believe Jesus is the best fucking version of humanity. There is much within *Heresy* that is simply an expression of things that Jesus said. I believe he, better than anyone, understood the need to call out power, corruption, and Systems of oppression. My critique of the institution is a desire to follow in his example, and, as he did, give a voice to the voiceless. My everyday role as a Rev is to simply reflect what he said. But I'm not here to convert or convince. I believe in the power of un- conditional love, seeing people united by our com- mon humanity. Those Systems that dehumanise us need to be called out and exposed, without fear.

Heresy is an expression of my own heart and journey, an honest reflection of how I see things. It won't be to everyone's taste, and that's okay. But, whatever you think of it, I hope you recognise that every work of poetry and prose contained in here comes from a place of integrity, words written by someone who is simply trying to say things as he sees it, without filter or fear.

One of my favourite writers is a German pastor and Nazi resistor called Dietrich Bonhoeffer. He was executed by the Third Reich on April 9 1945 at Flossenbürg concentration camp. He was a staunch critic of Hitler and the Nazi party, losing his life as a result. Yet he was also a fierce opponent of the German church. As Hitler rose to power, the German church wilted, lending its support to the Führer und Reichskanzler. Bonhoeffer was part of the Confessing Church, a movement of German Protestant Christians who opposed the Nazis. Yet Bonhoeffer would eventually despair, ashamed of the Confessing Church as it fell into nationalism and an inability to hold the government to account. Bonhoeffer refused to remain silent.

"Silence in the face of evil is itself evil," he once said. *"Not to speak is to speak. Not to act is to act."*

I see that same ecclesiastical silence and cowardliness today, alongside abuse and oppression that soaks the ground in the corridors of power. So, for some of us, our calling is to speak and act as best we can, to call it out, whatever the consequences.

Acknowledgements

Thank you to Perry and Jason who read early copies, highlighting weaknesses, and encouraging bravery to pursue the pieces that showed dark promise.

Thanks to Tia Ja'nae who saw the potential and told me to run with it. It is quite something when someone you admire and respect encourages you in your *own* craft.

My thanks to Alec and Uncle B. Publications for bringing this work into the world. I am truly grateful for your belief in my writing, and the passion for work that pushes the boundaries of accepted speech. Thank you.

To my friend, Sebastian Vice; thank you for believing in me, supporting my work, inspiring me, and writing a foreword of pure heart and beauty. Love you, man.

To Amy-Jean Muller for your words of encouragement, feedback, and kindness; thank you. You're an inspiration, so your willingness to support my work means everything.

The writing community on Twitter has been a source of real joy for me. I have found people who I have never met in person, but for whom I call my friends. The richness of conversation, the ways by which they help hone your craft, is invaluable. Thank you all.

Tom, Gemma, Autumn, I love you.

To Sarah, Grace, and Lizzie, my beautiful heretics; I love you. Thank you for your endless belief in me, the way you unconditionally love me, helping me become a better version of myself.

And to you, the reader. Thank you for reading this collection of heresies, encouraging me to shake the tree of institutional failure.

Our *somebodiness* truly matters.

About the Author

joehaward.co.uk
Twitter @RevJoeHaward

Rev Joe Haward is an author, poet, and heretic. Born into an Indian family, Joe was adopted with his identical twin brother, and grew up transracial in the UK.

Alongside two published nonfiction books, he works as a freelance journalist, challenging political, societal, and religious corruption, with articles regularly featured in the national news site, *Byline Times*.

His work can be found in various publications, where he writes horror, noir, and transgressive fiction. His poetry has also been nominated for the Pushcart Prize.

He is currently working on two horror novels and a novella. His debut horror novel, *Breath and Blasphemy* (Cinnabar Moth Publishing) will be released in 2023.

Indianapolis, Indiana

Printed in Great Britain
by Amazon

78134240R00068